Glass
Many Uses

No More Waste

This **jar** is made from **glass.**

I can **reuse** the jar.

This jar is made from glass.

I can reuse the jar.

This jar is made from glass.

I can reuse the jar.

This jar is made from glass.

I can reuse the jar.

This jar is made from glass.

I can reuse the jar.

This jar is made
from glass.

I can reuse the jar.

This jar is made from glass.

I can reuse the jar.

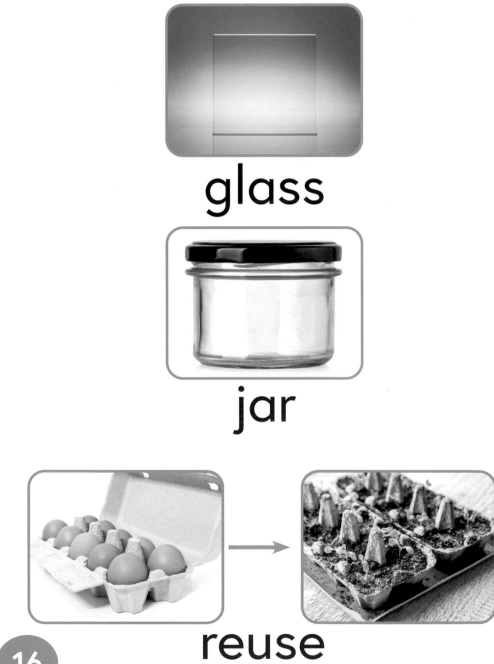

glass

jar

reuse